UNIDENTIFIED

SIGHING

OBJECTS

Baron Wormser

Baron Wormser (signature)

UNIDENTIFIED

SIGHING

OBJECTS

7/2015
Montpelier, VT

For Dick and Susan,
In friendship,
Love,
Baron

CavanKerry ◈ Press LTD.

CavanKerry Press Ltd.
Fort Lee, New Jersey
www.cavankerrypress.org

Publisher's Cataloging-in-Publication
(Provided by Quality Books, Inc.)

Wormser, Baron.
[Poems. Selections]
Unidentified sighing objects / Baron Wormser. --
First edition.
pages cm
Poems.
ISBN 978-1-933880-47-1

I. Title.

PS3573.O693A6 2015   811'.54
QBI15-600122

Cover art: *7th Grade*, Janet Wormser, private collection.
Cover and interior text design by Gregory Smith
First Edition 2015, Printed in the United States of America

CavanKerry Press is proud to publish the works
of established poets of merit and distinction.

CavanKerry Press is grateful for the support it receives from the
New Jersey State Council on the Arts.

This project is supported in part by an award from the
National Endowment for the Arts. To find out more about how
NEA grants impact individuals and communities, visit www.arts.gov.

Also by Baron Wormser

P O E T R Y

The White Words (1983)

Good Trembling (1985)

Atoms, Soul Music and Other Poems (1989)

When (1997)

Mulroney and Others (2000)

Subject Matter (2004)

Carthage (2005)

Scattered Chapters: New and Selected Poems (2008)

Impenitent Notes (2011)

P R O S E

Teaching the Art of Poetry: The Moves (co-author, 1999)

A Surge of Language:
Teaching Poetry Day by Day (co-author, 2004)

The Road Washes Out in Spring:
A Poet's Memoir of Living Off the Grid (2006)

The Poetry Life: Ten Stories (2008)

Teach Us That Peace: A Novel (2013)

For Janet

and to the memory of Donald Sheehan

For me alone, and only by myself,

within this heart, the poem's source,

between nothing and pure deed

—Paul Valéry, "Cemetery by the Sea"

(translated by Richard Miles)

Contents

I

. . . .

II

. . . .

III

. . . .

UNIDENTIFIED

SIGHING

OBJECTS

I

Falling Man

man fall, man fall
in bright air

angel rise
unheavy unmortal
spirit-fueled but

man fall burdened
tasked man
fall quickly
but / forever
in bright flightless moment
unheavy / pure /
illusion-fueled

flighted moment falling
time laughing
laughing at people
so heavy / unable
to rise / wingless
any bird better
in bright air
any angel

but man fall
woe-weighted
mind full
mouth screaming

pure
moment shattered
glass air / empty

man fall
into earth
good earth
no laugh no scream
well coming / like time
unheavy

but man fall
old story

Ode to George Hanson
(Easy Rider)

The *M* on his varsity sweater
Stands for Meaningful

Means over-educated small-town lawyer
Means ingratiating pain-in-the-butt boozer
Means understands the word *irony*
Means buried above ground
But lurching through the days
One pint to another / calendar of non-coincidences

Means he looks up at the midnight sky
Of unidentified sighing objects
Beckoning to drunken small-town lawyers
Wearing their varsity sweaters
And waiting for the earth to turn
In a different direction
Waiting for someone in Muleville to say something semi-smart

M stands for Mom
Marijuana Malthusian Momentary
This small-town lawyer tossed in the clink
Hoosegowed for his own good
Where he meets two LA hippies and splits
In search of the freedom which he knew
Without consulting any mystic text or atlas
Was not in Louisiana but somewhere inside him
Maybe next to his spleen or in back of his head
Where he can't see which was all the better
And called for a drink

Man has a beautiful legal smile
Charm money out of wallets
Women out of their clothes
Rain out of the clouds
But he blew it
Pouring bourbon on his shrewd thirst
Waking up in the clink
Looking around only half-bewildered / still on earth
Unlevitated by the Venusians
In their sighing objects

George Hanson small-town upright derelict lawyer
Buried above ground but walking and talking
And stalking a good time
Beaten lynched burned shot blown up
Sitting around the camp fire with two LA hippies
Explaining freedom
Lecturing the roaming lights in the night
The intelligent ones who live among us
But must be silent

Climate

Elyse, aged nine, worries about the ice
And polar bears with no place to go.
She lies in bed, alert to her fraught life;
Downstairs her mother weeps. The words *wife*,
Unfair, *too long* elongate and explode.

Elyse, aged nine, worries about the ice.
Her father tries to soothe *this endless strife*.
He talks like that, full of what he calls *woe*.

She lies in bed, alert to her fraught life
Where no beautiful animals entice
Little girls to live in homes of snow.
Elyse, aged nine, worries about the ice.

Igloos melt, mothers mutter, knife
The empty kitchen air, pace to and fro.
She lies in bed, alert to her fraught life.

What's been done is done not so much in spite
As fear—love marooned on a floe.
Elyse, aged nine, worries about the ice.
She lies in bed, alert to her fraught life.

The Present Tense of Jazz:
On a Photo by Roy DeCarava

Prim in a dress, a jumper,
A young white woman listens.
A few tables away, a young Negro man
Wearing a carefully knotted tie listens.

It must be past midnight.
Reason has headed home.
Only a few seekers still are up,
Tapping their internal feet

To the sound the planet would make
If it could riff a bit on its axis,
Invite a few stars down
To agglomerate the gravity.

Though bound by time and space
You can feel these two people
Aren't likely to speak.
They're listening.

That feels sad, the miserable starch of history
Floating on top of the unmelted pot,
But feels right and respectful too,
Since with each note their souls

Throb and faint,
Since as people
They didn't know they were so big and small,
So free despite themselves.

These two people in New
York City in the 1950s,
Not looking further than the moment,
Not touching one another

Which could make you weep for the loneliness
Of being in a body and praise it too:
Their dignity,
The music you can't hear but must be there.

Four

On Chandler Street in Baltimore a brick house
With a sectioned cement sidewalk, a maple tree,
A privet hedge, a rusting swing set.
I hold my breath but time rushes toward me.

*

On Chandler Street in Baltimore an old man
Gestures from a porch, his face bleak
With rage. "Goddamn you twice!" he hollers.
We stop our game of step ball, laugh till we shriek.

*

On Chandler Street in Baltimore the TV
Chirps like an electric cricket through the night.
"Suez Canal," I hear and wonder how
The earth can spin yet remain upright.

*

On Chandler Street in Baltimore it rains
To end the world, then ceases. I run outside
And splash in vast puddles—stomp, splat,
Stomp, splat. My life will not be denied.

Toward an Interstate Bodhisattva

The deal was that some morning
He'd look in the mirror and see
A craven, automatic face, well-earned
Contentment lodged in a well-shaved pelt,
An insurable success in spite of himself.

Goodbye to the Deer Park's internal cops,
Hello to automotive bop: fingers drumming
The dash, windows down, the hungry mind
An empty net, the accelerator
A nervy testament.

Each gas pump encounter
Or slice of pie in some fly-blown diner
A chance to spook someone new,
Who was—somewhere in there—alive
And waiting for a hard-traveling Buddha
To shatter the sad shell of misgiving.

He asked incautious questions
Then joked about his impertinence
As he placed his elbows on the counter,
Opened his green-blue eyes wide, repeated,
"Do you like your life?" and listened—
Spoon-stirring-the-coffee satori.

He marveled at the ragged, human flames,
Then threw them away,
Oblivion being the basic beauty.
He loved the scent and shape and stride and speech
And sex of every moving body.

If there is an aura beyond
The God-blessed blather of the exceptional nation,
If being free is the crucial vocation,
If legend is the spirit's compass
And every greeting is a road beginning,
Then his cordial flesh is everything.

Ode to the DC5

You read that the bassist in the Dave Clark Five has died
And think you didn't like the Dave Clark Five that much
They were peppy but not a whole lot more / overdoing
    their British
Notion of joy that wore thin in two minutes because it lacked
Sex and darkness that to the Brits' credit the Stones would
    soon provide

But you're sad anyway because you feel how even nostalgia
    slips away
How no one knows what George Washington was really like
We'll never sniff his breath or watch him clack his dentures
Or hear him say a word like "constitutional" and that hurts
Not because you're afraid of oblivion which would be silly

But because it's a drag how every story has to have the
    same ending
That's the beauty of poems though how they don't care
    about that
Poems just care about a teenage guy fumbling around with
    a bass
And then starting to get the plunk plunk hang of it
And meeting some other guys and starting a band or joining
    a band

And thinking "Hey, this is fun" and "Hey, I'm going to
    get laid"
And lots of good thoughts like that which come way
    before death

And that are immaterial because although the music isn't
    immemorial
It doesn't have to be because nothing has to be
Its failures are alluring as its successes maybe more so
    since genius

Is so rare the chance of some genius Liverpudlians coming
    together
Being about the same as you buying a Powerball ticket and
    winning sixty-three
Million dollars which still wouldn't buy immortality
But would give you a great stereo system to listen to the
    Dave Clark Five
Though after a while you'd realize you don't need a great
    stereo system

To listen to the Dave Clark Five / that in fact it makes the
    experience worse
Because you keep expecting something musical and that
    wouldn't be
The Dave Clark Five or its bassist thumping along like a
    flat tire
And that pimply *ésprit* feeling pretty bogus as the decades
    go down
In a hail of gunfire and grief or quiet bank accounts or
    grandchildren

But poetry doesn't care about that it's not an obituary
It's a lifetuary which in its way the Dave Clark Five was
Getting at how swell it is to be young and full of snappy
    sap and not knowing
Anything and not listening to anyone and being not much
    more

Than a gyrating body homing in on some homely lass who
    swoons with delight
At the opening bars of "Catch Us If You Can" even though
She knows the Beatles are way better than this stuff it
    doesn't matter
There are moments in life when anything will do and you
    just go with that
You say "Yes" to whatever is breathing hard in your face
Its breath maybe like George Washington's because he
    lived in some moments

Once upon a time and though he never heard an electric bass
    he must have
Wanted to rock out as a kid because kids always want to
    rock out
That's what their bodies are telling them / to pick up a
    bass or another person
Or a constitution or a nation and start rocking start
    plunking away
And feeling that though it's just you / some second-person
    figment that one

Uncharted day will dissolve into the listless ozone / it
    doesn't matter because
No one's counting how many ecstasy buttons you've pushed
    because one is enough

There Was a Duke Named Prospero

When I came to this island
The premise was clear:
Days ran round and round,
No hope for me here.

I learned to converse
With spirits and apes.
I stopped all complaining
About my spent fate.

Brackish or sweet,
The waters sustained me,
No genius or magic
But something paltry:

Time lisped in the breeze,
Age sang mute notes.
No fine ship arrived,
No mountebank told

Political lies.
No daughter, no dame.
Some nights I hear
The echo of fame—

A laughable tune.
Days run round and round.
I live almost freely,
Unsought, unfound.

Bearer

Imagine being the one who saw the wooden boat
Clatter ashore, the strange men step forward,
And heard their harsh voices in the morning wind.

Imagine calling your people together and beginning
To tell your vision: the day no longer a day
But a story fashioned by unwanted gods.

Imagine wringing sense out of what was senseless
Or a fraction of premonition: doom and demise
At last arrived, safe and stupidly sound.

They looked absurd, those bearded men who dropped
To their knees and intoned impossible words,
Who raised hands and eyes to the sharp-with-light sky.

Imagine being the one, the first, the bearer of tidings
That will transfigure death and ruin joy. Imagine
The one running back to his tribe, short forever of breath.

Mean Streets

Sal is a stand-up guy
But his brother Tony reads hardbounds
And quotes T. S. Eliot.

When they're out driving
They never get to where they intend.
They argue, whine, exclaim,

Root through ruined moments like
Someone tearing a drawer apart—
Where did I hide my secrets?

When they try to share memories,
Each has his fingerprint of the story:
You shoulda waited for me on the playground

I couldna waited on no account for you.
They glare and hiss
Like brawlers in a barroom standoff.

Tony chants, "The eyes are not here,"
And Sal gets weirdly pensive
As if Tony was onto something real.

When a boss asks Sal to do
Him a favor, you know the last act
Is about to occur. You watch them

In the car as they drive to whatever
Kickass Cavalry awaits them.
You can feel the rhythm of their jaws

As they snap their gum—
Batta batta batta—and can sense
They are one body, as they joke lightly

About a shirt or haircut or old girlfriend—
"She liked you best, you know that"—
Their brisk despair a relief.

Inquest

Real old.

Wife died coupla years back.

Hard goin' on.

I s'pose.

Lotta books and papers.

Needed a woman's touch.

Made a mess.

Guns do that.

Guess by now I should know.

Guess.

Wonder what the cat thought.

Do they?

Course they do.

I had a dog once.

Don't start in.

Old hippie?

Hippies gotta be young
That's what makes 'em hippies.

That musta been his wife.

Coulda been.

Pretty woman.

Don't step there.

Life's a beautiful meaningless
Gift.

Say what?

Ode to the Great Sad Artist
(Diane Arbus)

Look look look
Around her neck
The noose of the camera
Implacable indifferent dull
Magical
Like a porter at a gate
Interceding
She stands at a gate
She carries the world on her back
A pack of unwholesome toys
The porter smiles sneezes sneers
Take this she says
See that
The porter yawns

What is beautiful is awful
What is awful is beautiful
Perhaps Goethe said that and a teacher told her
She holds the camera to her chest
Can it hear her?
Oh cheap omni-presence!
How does she dare to cramp the unholy world
To usher existence into a pew
To tailor the measurements of infinite space
Hush she says
Hush

The tall man the thin man the fat woman the short woman
The bearded woman the elevator man the flower woman
The human wreck the human pincushion the human map
The seal boy the wolf girl the chicken man the bear woman
The woman who is a man the man who is a woman
Everyone walks down a street
Everyone goes home at day's end
And lights something against the night
While the great sad artist
Welcomes the absence of clarity
Inserts a flashbulb in her apparatus
Sits at the kitchen table
And broods over the dreams of strangers
The grief that tunnels under the skin
The smooth mask of perturbation
The bodily home that is no home

She will find everyone out
She will hold a moment
Who has done that?
Achilles Hector Gilgamesh Roland
Who has held a moment
And not let go?

She can be her own myth
But she cries and puts her head down on the table
There is no one to cheer her up
Except a machine that makes everything worse
That piles woe upon adroit woe
While she scrambles up the side of a building
A bridge a face a cloud
Fearful but alert
Not Achilles Hector Gilgamesh Roland
But a woman in a dress

Click click click
Everything must be lost
All this careful finding must be lost
Only that makes the great sad artist smile
Only that

Exhilaration Blues
(Last Days of the Berlin Wall)

Gaping tourists everywhere:
  Leicas, Nikons, Minoltas.
That's the way it is now. As Uncle says,
Life's become a spectator sport.
Even then
When the streets were silly with people—
Matrons and schoolboys, butchers and writers—
Someone's trying to nudge history
A bit to the left or right for composition's sake,
Diddling with the light, the drama of millimeters.
Someone's explaining gravely to the surprised
  how there are no surprises.

Gretel was shouting her soul out
For her father who was tripped up by the Stasi
In the mid-Sixties and drank himself
To death a few gray years later.
Some guy in Levis sidled up to her.
"You're a sweet piece of goods under any ideology."
"Thus, capitalism begins," she sniffed back at him.

Karl said it was the Woodstock of anger.
You could see it in the way people danced,
  that twitchy, beleaguered kick:
Not the stateside sensory pandemonium,
  the Hendrix waft of freaky hope,
But something that crackled and lurched, edgy yet
  jolly too, like an air-escaping balloon.

On the mornings after, pensioners sifted through litter.
Policemen prodded the stunted embers of duty.
In a mild wind two placards tumbled:
  "Brecht has finally died."
  "Brecht will live forever."
Auntie told Gretel a dab of horseradish
  in schnapps could cure the sorest throat.
Gretel said she didn't mind being hoarse.
  It was her passion and her choice.

II

Haircut (1956)

Men must be mundane,
                    their virile vanity veiled
In crew cuts, critique
                    of hair, head honed
To thin thrust
                    of follicles, fine flatland.
Extreme the empty edge
                    but Bob the barber
Sharpened shears, shook
                    ample aprons, aimed
Tonic and talked TV,
                    Ike, illness, invasions
Of countries by Communist killers,
                    while the wealth of weeks
Fell formlessly, the fix
                    of lessened locks lightly
Combed, the cunning clack
                    and whack whelming wavy
Sensuousness, Samson's strength
                    beggared, bound, buzzed.

Patchwork

The remnants of love come down to
An old calico cat sitting in the early morning
Before our bedroom door croaking
Feed me
You fed me yesterday
And whatever came before yesterday
And the Boy Scout knife I carry
Though it is not a knife, file, letter opener,
Scissors, or can opener but
An ugly faded green plastic and metal
Relic of something I never cared for anyway
But thought I should.

And your sleeping face
One of countless, present-yet-absent masks,
A breathy flower,
Eyes closed, sedate, sightlessly staring
Into the heights of nothingness
Until some memory spooks your soul—
The fourth-grade cloakroom,
Two bigger girls who have it in for you.

And the patchwork quilt on our bed—
Our saving genius.
Frayed and lumpy
Assembled by patient hands
From the unnoticeable, from cloth
That started out sunny as sight,
Confident matter ending with a wince—

Cat whining, knife dull,
Your face mortally still, slandered by oblivion—
Yet become a whole:
Something larger, if not grander.

Ode to the Ghost Dancers

Busy with time, I forget out-of-time.
How to recall?
The stars shuffle in their recondite heaven.
To hear them I must be still.
To hear them
I have to open my beleaguered head.
How much money did I make today?
The spirits watch and grimace.

Thousands of Indians shuffle their feet,
A thin yet supple sound.
If you stand outside Walmart, Taco Bell, Eddie Bauer,
The shilling hearts of the fluorescent republic
And are very still
Above the cars starting people prattling radios
     broadcasting
You can feel the tremor of moccasin feet shuffling
     not stopping
Dancing past exhaustion past hope and hopelessness
To a place out-of-time but in life
The concise moments of crickets beavers buffalo on a
     lush prairie
Ravens talking
"Have you seen the Indians?
They are almost all dead but they have plenty of ghosts."

No ghosts for sale
In Walmart, Taco Bell, Eddie Bauer,
Only those hungry ghosts
Buying twelve packs of paper towels, extra sauce,
     signature twill shirts

Chanting
Walmart Taco Bell Eddie Bauer
Walmart Taco Bell Eddie Bauer
Walmart Taco Bell Eddie Bauer

I forget how many died for this.
How many were scalped, eviscerated, speared, arrowed.
Their ghosts are angry too
But the Indians continue to dance.

The troops ride into the encampment at Wounded Knee
And start shooting.
Screams.
Many screams.

Everyone moves on, nothing comes back
But like sun and clouds and stars
The spirits are undeterred.
They hear the shuffling feet,
The cries that pierce the squander of grief.

High School Students Reciting Keats, Donne, et al. (2011)

The premise—words sent forth—is a promise,
This brittle length of sound informing bones,
Eyes and most—your voice—so that the throb
Becomes you, so that intimation

Holds you, a perfected finger on
Time's folio that gives the wan air shape.
"Go not" and "unravished" and "love" and mere "oh"
Announce wry bravado, heart-dealt cheer

That later won't be rued or disabused
But will remain that weird stuff of poetry
That each young person has seized and now speaks,
As if a life might be parsed in lines,

As if the moat between selves might be bridged
And what exists as flash or glint persist.

Two Places

1. Paris, France (1940)

A little man—no one you'd notice normally—
Hops up and down. Behind loom stone buildings.
Paris is his.
              Once, kings and cardinals
Decreed magnificence. Who knows how many
Were crushed or fell? Those graves are ancient.
                          The bells
Of Europe darkly knell. People flee
On bikes and wagons, in cars and trains. People
Walk as quickly as they can. Who knows
How many days remain?
                 Once, the little man
Stood outside of history, muttering, gnashing
His hatred, singly bent on overcoming.
Once, such a little man would have been crushed
By kings and cardinals and their buildings.
Now, he is the shrieking star of destiny.

2. South Paris, Maine (1944)

A slightly stooped farmer in a flannel shirt
And suspenders stands beside the post office
And breathes in the tang of an autumn morning—
Wood smoke and frost, winter coming.

No letter from Robert Junior. Three weeks.
The farmer knows everyone on this street
And they know him. He wanders over to Vi's
For coffee and maybe a slice of apple pie.

He's always liked pie in the morning, after
Milking, something to sink his teeth into.
People ask him if he's gotten a letter.
He doesn't blame them. He rests his chin

In his palm, then sips black Sanka slowly,
Avoids the newspaper. He knows his history.

Historical Painting:
The Demise of Andy Warhol

The canvas
  (a pre-neon medium used for centuries)
    brims with manic strokes.

Death,
  that Old Master,
Dogs it, an expressionist
Whose agile, spitfire hand notes
Each hidden nerve of the bland terrorist.

Somehow disappointing
  that the flash of cameras,
    for instance,
Cannot dislodge the sullen body's flaws.
A dumb tumult severs the trance
Of self-importance.
        The lower laws

Prevail as—
  to give him credit—
    call-me-Andy knew:
Bored wit and the comic art
Of artlessness, that was America's true
Confession and better than some old farts

Addressing a relic of inwardness.
Depth is what surface designs.
An image is the halo of success.
Fifteen minutes is a lot of time.

Everyone mediaizes, gossiping.
Money has no lachrymose regrets.
In the painting
  a yawning orderly looks in
At the skewed, blond wig
  of a lapsed portrait.

Ode to Speech

Still fumbling with words, as if attempted eloquence
Could preserve you in my backward sight,
As if your death held other deaths at bay,
I see you emerging from the Olds Eighty-Eight,
A bandage on your head that the scarf you bought
At Liberty of London on your one trip abroad
Doesn't quite cover and you shrunken inside
Your winter coat and moving very slowly,
Tottering would be the word, though you
Were only forty-seven and trying to form a smile
Of some sort, a *desperate* smile, a smile
To rid you of pain and the weariness that
Eats my very bones, a smile to show you were
Fighting back as you taught me to fight back
When the world taunted me.
                              You halted on the sidewalk
As if to take in the cold breeze,
As if, after weeks away, weeks in a small white room,
It was a pleasure, the raw January air, how
It shoved and gnawed at a body's modest warmth.

You looked around slowly, your neck creaking,
It lately having done little more
Than prop up your cancer-besieged head,
And tried to say something, maybe about
The sky or house or our German shepherd Lady
Who wagged her tail bravely, but no words
Came out, none, only a rueful blankness,
More of that stolid fumbling that was
The ruin of each laugh and kiss and exclamation.

You seemed bewildered to be there, to be alive,
To be expected to respond when all
That lay in front of you was your coming to a bed
And waiting—patient and impatient—for what the words
Nothing more to be done signified.

You'd told me you'd overheard those words—
One intern informing another.

                                              I love you all, you said
Then on the sidewalk to the dog and your husband
And us children but you didn't smile, your words
Were quiet and grave like the words in a speech
But from the depths of words, their blind insides.

Praise Poem

The years tucked in
Like happy drowsy children—
What a good life it's been!
Time bearing garrulous days
The sky quick with sculpted mist

Earth redolent with rain
Galactic habit banging out rhythm
And you moored in the murmur of tides
And pulses, warbling "Sunrise, Sunset"
And loving it despite

The Buddhist texts you've read
Revealing delusions bred
By attachment, the mind
Clutching what is not there
But that's the beauty

Of samsara, it strings you along
And you assent, believing
Each idle, succulent lie or not
Believing but choosing fool-
Hardiness, scanning how-to books,

Sutras, rational tomes of reasonable doubt,
Existence a bewitching read
In which you turn not-infinite pages
Overwhelmed but upright,
Savoring the authored moment.

Upon Hearing of the Death
of a Former Lover

Again the dawning flush of your pale flesh,
You undressing slowly, back to me,
Then turning and smiling—wry and winsome.
"What you wished?" you asked. Not a question.

I stood in reply. Then the full skein of you
Rubbing against me and the smooth static
Of our different-but-one bodies.
Passion that even now, decades later,

Makes memory whimper. I pace
On the back porch among shovels and returnables,
Hear your meter of grunts and gasps. I stop,
Protest your name like a faith.

Port Authority, 1969

"Lez chicks?" the pocked Puerto
Rican man who seemed to me to be
Somewhere out there in the tundra
Of Late Middle Age asked
As I headed from my bus toward
Some distant exit in the Port Authority
Whose name always confused me
Since there were no boats or docks.

"No thanks, sir," I replied. "I'm going to hear
The Allman Brothers at the Fillmore East,"
As if that somehow explained something.

I kept walking as did he.

"One thing, sonny, I want to tell you
Is call me any fool thing but not 'sir.'"

In front of a staircase we both stopped.
I eyed his hair—dosed with tonic
And slicked back à la 1956.

"You understand me, sonny? I'm under
The heel not above the heel. You get it?"
Half-earnest, half-contemptuous,
He leered appropriately.

"Yes, sir," I answered.

He regarded me with visceral wonder.

"One thing I forget, sonny, is *stupid*.
No matter how much I see it and I fucking
Live it, I forget."
He shook his head. A lock of oily hair
Fell forward.

A guy in a business suit edged up to us.
"You, Hector?" the guy asked.

I wanted to yell something like "How much?"
Or "How long?" Or "What the hell happens?"
But the moment dissolved into the ugly lights
And trash on the floor and the night outside,
Minatory, the way night is supposed to be.

A Call

Reva's brother Saul is on the phone,
I heard she's dying. I want to make amends.
I say nothing, wonder how time can atone

And what is the sound of God's dial tone—
An urgent beep or New Age jazz blend?
Reva's brother Saul is on the phone

And I need to do more than stupidly moan.
I need to ask what it is he intends:
I say nothing, wonder how time can atone.

When a body dies the soul is most alone
As it awaits its unknowable friends.
Reva's brother Saul is on the phone.

His voice is a river, a sour drone,
A satchel of rue, a star caught in a lens.
I say nothing, wonder how time can atone.

Reva is beyond the pale of words. No one
Can seize her heart, no one can reach her end.
Reva's brother Saul is on the phone.
I say nothing, wonder how time can atone.

Two Failed Marriages

In her dream two men sit at a bare table.
Mr. First starts complaining but about what?
Something about a rubber duck,
He's lost his rubber duck and someone—

He draws himself up when he says this
Like a taut vertical elastic—someone
Is going to pay for this. Mr. Second
Sneers politely. You have to look

Carefully because he doesn't seem
To possess anything as accomplished
As a face. He doesn't talk; instead
Frog-like *oofs* issue from his chest.

Yes! There is a big mouth in his chest
Between his nipples. Suddenly, the table
Begins to levitate. The rubber duck man
Claps with abrasive glee;

The *oofer* pretends nothing is happening.
Then a bewitched candle is floating through
What must be air though no one is breathing
Or laughing or crying or singing or anything.

Syllabic Dithyramb:
Shea Stadium, 1965

The deep sky broods
The ground shakes
Girl-women cry
The Fab Four have a date

Rocked-out shrieks
Time ending
Orgasmic sighs
Girl-women cry

Terror-like joy
Girl-women cry
Transfixed
Sort of die

Girl-women cry
Tear their clothes
Pull their hair
Faint but rise

Mouths distended
By Eros
Girl-women cry
A pagan rite

Electrified
Virgin lust
Untouched ache
Girl-women cry

Free but not free
Girl-women cry
Take me
Satyrs take me

Ode to Basketball

"Don't bring that weak shit into my kitchen,"
P-Man tells Spice as the latter tries to drive right
With no space / only his unemployed will at work
In the urban twilight where Werner strolls and broods
About his homeland and how he wants to return and doesn't /
Ambivalent as an ambidextrous point guard swinging the ball
Left right left right psyching out his opponent and himself

Unlike the guy in the wheelchair watching these proceedings
And saying to all averted eyes, "My body is a broken temple,"
As P-Man arcs a jumper over Spice's long arms that
    bounces off
The back of the rim / one more misplaced thought in a galaxy
    of them
Like his longing for Sonya who keeps telling him he needs
    "to get
His shit together" which is what he's trying to do when he
    plays ball
Except she thinks ball is play stuff for kids not men
    and women

While Werner sends home e-mails each day about the game
In the asphalt park and how "America is the home of the
    homeless" which is
His way of saying he can't go home because there's
    something hopeless
Yet earnest—*hoffnungslos aber ernsthaft*—keeping him here
That goes beyond the guy in the wheelchair

Who's become a friend of sorts both of them kibitzing about
    how Spice
Is gaining / how he's learning to move without the ball

The way the coaches tell you instead of standing round
    waiting
For shit to happen / a waste of time according to Sonya who
    is studying
Fashion design and intends to change at least one world /
    Paris Milan New York
Outstretched at her non-sneakered feet or so she tells
    P-Man after
They have sex and are lying on his thin mattress in his sad
    broken-window-shades
Bedroom just as he starts to boogie off to sleep to dream of
    the NBA
Launching himself over bodies benches arenas headed for
    something like glory /

That not being a word he uses in his daily parlance it being a
    word someone
Like Werner is prone to / missing as *ein Deutscher* does those
    centuries that brayed
And cantered in the presence of majesty / a homeland—*eine
    Heimat*—that he can
Pine for safely since it won't be his warrior grave that Time
    won't salute /
It won't be his sense of how shooting fouls on a Wednesday
    afternoon is okay
As anything and better than most / the sky a vexed cloud
    jumble and the air
Unhealthy but ripe with that city tang of bus exhaust and
    bustling bodies

Emitting little doses of perspiring feeling / like stutter steps
toward some
Distant emotional hoop / like a fashion designer standing
before a cadre
Of cameras and smiling a real fake smile and thinking of
some guy
She knew once how she loved him and how he never got off
his ass
Even though he could leap through the air and seem to fly
but there
Was no place to fly to no homeland no wheelchair no nothing
only a ball

III

Joy

To scoop up a scrap of feeling
That falls from the gusty October sky

A raw little thing like a bare hatchling
Or fresh bloodstain

The air thick with ocher and violet
As if an abstract expressionist

Had taken hold of a cloud and soaked it
Till it bled ghost tears

Then brayed with crafty giddiness
At art's prodigal counter-punch

A bray the cars take up out of impatience
For they must be elsewhere and soon

And this moment
Is only a mental tunnel

More failed history
Though when a woman turns

Her head sideways and sees one
Of those slim trees the city plants

Clinging to a few last leaves
As if they were dignity itself

It's hard not to squirm with admiration
Lift weary hands off the wheel

And yell to the stooped goggle-eyed guy
On the sidewalk leaning to catch something

"Don't pocket it. Let it grow."
The guy looks up big incredulous eyes

Big ears too and like
The Wandering Jew he softly groans.

Ode to Matter

"Here's to Nothing," a person says and hoists a pale ale.
The person appraises the Stevens-like riches of Something:
Hammocks, Hammers, Hummers, Hymns.
The universe stutters its casual gifts:
Wind's shifting harmonies,
Light bestowing green pleasance.

"Down the hatch," the person says.
Glug, glug drifts on the vanishing breeze.

A person can't see that hatch nor can the universe
Despite the mojo of conceptual language
That creates entities out of empty air,
Existential confetti a person adorns his or her psyche with,
Coordinates for a possible personal map,
A vacation spot for cosmic ennui.

"Can't see me," the person says, which is untrue
Unless it's night, the relative absence of light,
Or the person lives in said universe which is too big to see
Which dwarfs a person dwarfs even wind and light
The universe throbbing at every frequency / a big atonal radio
Something John Cage might have invented but couldn't have
Because he was a person hoisting a pint of sound
And hiccupping to the surrounding silence / a serenade of sorts
The universe could never hear.

"Sad," the person says as car alarms klaxons sirens electric
Things zing, ping, and brrrring.
The word disappears, a missing face hijacked by

Some estranged parent bound for points beyond points
Except that disappearance, as the posters in the post office
     attest,
Holds a life, an era, an eon, though it's best to stop there
Before the frame gets too big,
Sit by the wayside and tell tales to travelers
Burnt by the sun and harried by the wind.

"Once there was a universe," a person tells the travelers.
Everyone likes a story that starts like that,
Auguring orphans, queens, potions, and a view
Of the inconsequence and breadth of a human life
That is not unwanted though tolerable typically
Only in small fantastic doses.

Wind disrupts the person's just-combed hair.
"This is more than I can take," the person says.
"There is always wind. How is that?
Is someone speaking to me? Is the wind a word?"

The person gets up as if to go but knows that story,
Knows how there is no leaving, how there is only
This shuffling of a one-suit deck, this passing of
The baton from one insubstantial hand to another,
Death being the father, mother, sister, brother,
The compost bin replete with bread heels, soggy mung
Bean sprouts, grass clippings, apple peels,
And a fine black humus ideal for growing
Tomatoes, cucumbers, peppers—every exuberant
Aggregation of molecules sub-molecules sub-sub-
     anti-molecules,
Discriminations that trace the ghost of a ghost into
A vast no-sided hall where wind sings and light sighs.

"Guess I'll hang around," the person says,
"And see how the compost is doing."
The person waits again for a reply.
That's how persons are.
Within the black plastic bin a worm greets
A bit of what once was a cabbage leaf.
Elsewhere a star begins to fade.

Sanctify

He waved a Bible—Voice bequeathed to earth—
An un-calm gesture between threat and gift
Shattering this breathy moment's mirth,
Evoking whited shades of eternal worth
That might heal each soul-starved rift.

He waved a Bible—Voice bequeathed to earth—
Promising a better, more diligent birth,
One that gathered epiphanic uplift
(Shattering this breathy moment's mirth)
Replacing the belligerent daily dearth
With joy indifferent to matter's shifts.

He waved a Bible—Voice bequeathed to earth—
Then, tongue tapping, quaked, the demon unearthed,
Clutching the Book, a wordy raft adrift,
Shattering this breathy moment's mirth
With what he feared—the cross lukewarm, unnerved
Before his own coffin-thin width.

He waved a Bible—Voice bequeathed to earth—
Shattering this breathy moment's mirth.

Jerry Lee Lewis at Nuremberg

In unreal time, as when a head dices up decades
Centuries millennia
While slowly sluicing into the nether bog of sleep,
Jerry Lee Lewis, also titled "The Killer,"
For among other things, his pianistic prowess,
Appears at Nuremberg in a stiff, wide-lapel suit
He could have bought at Lansky's in Memphis
If he was from Memphis but he wasn't,
Standing there with that too-cool hairdo
To confront the modest panoply of Nazis who
Are standing in for many Nazis
Who are there to take the rap and glad in their
We-are-the-superior-race way to do that since
It was a service to Aryans to cleanse the earth of scum,
Which by implication included musicians
Humping pianos and thirteen-year-old cousins
While braying like country-western-boogie-woogie banshees.
Jerry Lee has no time to dig this whacked-out ideology.
He doesn't give a teenage shit about the tatters
Of their goose-stepping, *sieg-heil*-ing murder machine.

What matters is the sweet dross in his love-exercised mind—
An undressed woman and some get-down hands
Hurricaning a keyboard, which is what a mind should hold,
So that when Göring starts in with his witty repartee
Jerry Lee says, "You are one sad motherfucker,"
And the world, for once, gets what it is to be American
And unafraid of what anyone thinks, especially some
Nazi slime ball who believes he's better than anyone else
Because he's from Europe and has a lot of unhappy history

Up his vicious asshole that got made into more history that
Soldiers like my uncle Nathan paid for with his life
On the beach at Anzio, his precious blood vanishing
Into the grievous sands of silence.

Göring says something smug but Jerry Lee is busy
Waggling his eyes around the courtroom.
No chicks or pianos.
Being serious is fucking boring.
Being serious has killed a lot more people than not being
    serious.

The dream ends here.
In Hollywood time, Spencer Tracy is talking about
"The real complaining party in this courtroom," which is
    "civilization."
Everyone nods at this large last word.
It sounds good like maybe you could use it in a song,
Each syllable taut yet sibilant in its brief articulate leap,
Though it doesn't rhyme with much,
Though it feels like some wish, something badly out of touch.

Don't Send Us Any Poems about Poetry

Another hallooing species of pathos—
Dewy assertion meeting tactless fact
While some sad or puissant self stands
Downstage muttering about flowers, bread,
Time's witless, unsigned aggression pact
As acerbic gods rain shit, war,
Unrequited everything on one more lover's
Brimming, aggrieved, near-desperate head.

Every moment a triumph in the sweepstakes of
Random, abiding feeling—fingers clutching
Air, umbrella handles, wet matches
Meant to set afire glacial mysteries,
The whole rank savor of unwanted memory
Seeping through words, terminably.

Southern California Ode (1970)

We were living in Orange County in a beach house
With another miniscule beach house behind us where a very
    crew cut
Guy lived who was a Mormon and worked for the FBI
    neither of
Which we knew because he never spoke to us
Beyond "Hi, sir" and "Hi, ma'am" which from some other party
Might have seemed sarcasm, given that we were younger by
    ten or so years
And in our unadulterated male and female ways
In the free-love lane of the sexual highway, but wasn't,
As our neighbor Mike, who sold us pot and often shared a
    taste of his latest parcel,
Informed us while we toked up and babbled about the taut
Underpinnings of various unraveling anomies before ending
    up a few hours later
Mentally supine and staring at the sedated sky.

We never could decide which paranoia to supplicate:
Smoking dope not many feet away from an FBI guy
Or having a queasy intimation that he was in some separate
    reality
In which Kennedy still was freaked out about Castro and
    the sternest task
A G-man faced was to bust Mafiosi for tax delinquency. Or
    maybe
Despite his crew cut and his girlfriend whom we saw on the
    weekends
In a one-piece bathing suit and who was cute
In a desperately perky Doris Day way, he too

Was smoking dope and having visions if not of Cody then
Of J. Edgar twinkletoeing across a dance floor in lingerie
    mufti
And cooing, "I love a communist who knows how to kiss."

You can tell me America isn't paranoid, that all the people
    with arsenals
In their closets are just collectors, but I won't believe you
Because one typically sun-struck afternoon the girlfriend
    banged on
Our door screaming, "He's got a gun! He's going to kill me!"
    and sobbing
Like her face was going to come off but he didn't kill her, he shot
Himself—one comic strip "bam" a few minutes later while
    we were offering
Downers to the girlfriend whose name was Trish and who
    was, she confided,
"Not ready to die."

                    We sat there waiting for some annunciation but
There wasn't any, the silence like the desert east of LA—
    endless and hopeless.
There wasn't going to be anything unless it was what Mike
    in his opulent
Stoner moments called "society," that swanning firmament
    of film stars, cars,
Ball players, money, Jesus, and fears of fearsome Reds
    while the FBI infiltrated
Panhandling hippies who proclaimed along with a plea for
    spare change that
Everything was cool as a topless babe lolling by a swimming
    pool waiting
For Jack to show—his head unexploded, his smile an ever
    beneficent glow.

Someone

At the funeral (pan-denominational,
Replete with folk songs, chants, and spirituals)
Asks in a voice that hovers too tensely
Above the bare ground of pity if her grown
Schizophrenic son is "in attendance."

I remember staying up late with her over cups
Of Bancha tea and her telling me once
In downtown Boston she recognized Timmy,
Whom she hadn't seen for at least three years,
Picking through a trash bin near Filene's for empties.
Transfixed, she gaped, didn't move.
Always she loved him, she told me
But part of her had come to feel that love was vapor—
Or worse, elicited more bereft trouble
As it sought to smooth impossible wrinkles.

He seemed serene, carefully sorting through
The late twentieth-century debris of Whopper boxes,
Lifestyle sections, plastic, and cellophane.
He wore a green sweater she had knit for him,
A crewneck that was badly stretched
And even from across the street looked stiff with sweat
And worse. Still, she felt at peace, done with the hoodoo
    of hope.
His gestures reminded her of a surgeon.
She walked away.

She's dead now is what our presence says.
Her son isn't here today.

We press to our chests some semblance of memory,
Some clumsy internal melody.
And sing, if not well, then with feeling
For our avowed diminishing.

An Island Romance (Maine)

Imagine everything being in place.
I don't mean only the pins in the drawers
Though I mean that too but I mean
Your feelings—not squashed or pruned—
But right in place and everything around
You in place too. That's what
An island is, that kind of chance.

I know you can say that everything *is*
In place already, that trees can't dance
And birds shed feathers not leaves
And that it's the rightness of place that counts—
And it is—but love gets mixed in here,
The love between men and women,
Husband and wife that we say
We understand the way we understand
Anything that we do over and over
Till it becomes a kind of weather
But I'm talking about a man and woman
Living together more than forty years
On an island and no one else there.
I'm talking about a real man—
Black hair, medium height, a trace
Of a limp on his left side—and a real
Woman—blonde hair, high voice, small hands—
Who sometime in the late '40s—how about
'47?—came to Sheep Island which no
Longer had any sheep and which had gone
Back to spruce and built a house of cement

He rowed over bag by bag from the big island
And of those spruce he cut and fit
Until it looked like a fairy tale house—
Each window casing made by hand,
Each pane set in the sash just so,
Each window placed for the fullest light.

He fished enough and she knitted sweaters
And they lived and people wondered but
They weren't bothering anyone. They had as
Much claim to live on a place that no one
Wanted to live on as anyone. When you saw
The two of them together in Cundy's store
As often as not they were holding hands.
They were neat looking—combed and clean—
But you felt a little uneasy because
You felt how deep love could go,
That it could pull you off into a world
Where you stopped caring about what
Others thought, that the merest touch
Of another hand could make your blood simmer
And softly growl with feeling that had to go off
By itself it was that strong.

                    They never invited
Another soul out there ever. They got older
And they used the boat with the engine
Instead of rowing over but they still held
Hands and lived in that house we
Could picture because we had seen it
In children's story books. That's why
The blather about years and bags
Of cement is just blather—the sorry lint

Of facts, the *believe* in make-believe.
These two people had the sea for ears
And the sky for eyes and when they
Came together as man and woman
The pity of fathoms, the cold ocean notes
That sang outside their windows seemed to waver.

I know about age and death, as did they,
But think of the mornings when they sat
By the cook stove they'd hauled out there,
When he came back from the out of doors and she
Put down her handiwork and they sat there
With each other, drinking their tea and
Their mouths making little in-drawing sounds
And their putting their cups down
And how the fullness of being alive
Was the rich heat of their imagining.

For Marion Stocking

My wife and I spent a pleasantly boozy evening
Browsing your yearbooks—Mount
Holyoke, Class of '43 and Phi Beta
Though you never would brag.

Here and there, stuck between pages
Were wedding notices you had clipped.
"Everyone married a lieutenant.
I wanted to study more."

Those weren't the days—
Stables for the horsy set and formals
That were "the near side of tedium."
Principles of Prosody stole your heart.

When you said you never read a novel
Anymore, I gasped.
"But surely John Updike."
"Ah, yes, he writes delicious poems."

In the morning we found you sorting through submissions.
"Listen to this," you almost crowed.
"Fuck you, bitch editor, who never likes my poems!"
You smiled grandmotherly.

Books ruled your Maine roost.
Light glimmered off the inlet.
You rattled the rocks in your whiskey—ping, ping:
Each day a versification.

On Narrative

If I could add the days and make a sum
Of moments—faces pulled, unpulled, peas
Pushed around a forlorn plate, jokes
Gotten, ungotten, the taking in of each tree,
Building, chair, strand of hair lying
In the bathroom sink—I wouldn't be human
In the sense we use that word as a form
Of gauze over a large but approximate wound,

A gesture of dismissal and acceptance
Adding up (there is that notion again!)
To bludgeoned wisdom dispensed too free of charge
To all and semi-sundry. "I can't do the math,"
I told the teacher and left the room, though
At once I looked about and started counting.

Not Jim

Cool June night
Moon somewhere between half
And three-quarters
Makes me think of James—
Not Jim—with whom I ran
The mile relay in high school
And who died three years later
In Vietnam in '68.

Endless moons he did not live to see,
His graceful body ripped by a mine
To smithereens.
When he enlisted, he called me up,
"It's somethin' to do."

Once after a meet when we were
Waiting for the bus to come,
He told me that
Thinking made him tired.
He told me I ran as though
I was thinking.
"Don't think," he instructed me.
He called himself "Fast Ass."

What was isn't,
But I can see him—
Stretching in his warm-ups,
Jogging in place, laughing.

I squeeze the phantom years,
Savor their empty wine.

Moon slides across the sky.
Slowly.

Poem Beginning with
a Line by Hölderlin

Night comes full of stars and not greatly concerned about us,
A line to quote not about a human beginning or end
But the seemingly steady middle,

The place that placidly looks backwards and forwards,
Quoting poetry, explaining to someone about Hölderlin's genius
While regarding the moon as if the moon were about to speak

As if piety could add more life to life
As if negligence did not matter and the person to whom
The line is quoted, a lover or friend, could nod or move closer

And purr some soft agreement / words that floated out
Toward what Hölderlin might have called the heavens
Because he was fond of the old mysteries that mocked

In their dignified way—a sonorous toast at midnight—
The middle with its lists of purposes
Because night comes and anyone who looks up

Can realize how the background to our thoughts is the
    foreground
Of something so vast that only a poet / someone
Who is not afraid to lose him or herself can speak lines

With that quiet force that goes
Beyond any overtures of sincerity and that in its lilting
Opaque way—little concerned with us—emanates its own

Cold light that does not so much illuminate but casts
A blessing on the grandeur of indifference, a calm nod
To the workings of vastness that stir within us when we stop

Beneath the night sky and do not move on
Or say something but stay in our place whatever that is
And calmly nod / full of the night within us.

Ring: Wedding Anniversary Poem

Fingerhold who does not start or end,

I need you, little weight that speaks *sotto*
Voce for the consequent mood inside me.
Blank as virtue, your persistence warns—
However it may seem, a circle is not simple.

I fall and rise; you turn flat purpose
To luster, encompass flesh, bone, and nerve
But never merge. Idly, I slip you off,
Thinking, not thinking. You exhale calmly.

Pale indent, vacant moon, I salute you.
How stern you are! How indifferent! Nothing
Like love yet I adore you the more
Who are precise and decorous, bestowed and untold.

Leaving

Not to be here anymore, not to hear
The cat's fat purring, not to smell
Wood smoke, wet dog, cheap cologne, good cologne,
Not to see the sun and stars, oaks

And asters, snow and rain, every form
I take mostly for granted, makes me sad
But pleased to be writing down these words,
Pleased to have been one more who got the chance

To participate, who raised his hand although
He didn't know the answer or understand
The question. No matter. The leaving makes me sad;
So much was offered, so freely and completely.

Acknowledgments

Thanks to the editors of the following publications in which versions of some of these poems first appeared: *Stosvet, New World Writing, Post Road, Manhattan Review, Puckerbrush Review, Beloit Poetry Journal, Iron Horse Literary Review, Florida Review, Down East, Poetry Salzburg Review, Café Review, Brilliant Corners.*

"Toward an Interstate Bodhisattva" is dedicated to David Cappella. "Jerry Lee Lewis at Nuremberg" is dedicated to Glenn Marcus.

Thanks to the Vermont Studio Center for the opportunity to work on these poems in a sustaining environment.

Thanks to the people at CavanKerry Press who helped make this book possible: Joan Cusack Handler, Teresa Carson, Dawn Potter, and Starr Troup. Special thanks to Jeanne Marie Beaumont for her editorial input.

CavanKerry's Mission

CavanKerry Press is committed to expanding the reach of poetry to a general readership by publishing poets whose works explore the emotional and psychological landscapes of everyday life.

Other Books in the Notable Voices Series

Both the text and the display type for this book were set in the Century Schoolbook typeface, which was designed in 1919 by Morris Fuller Benton. Century type faces are known for their great legibility—so much so that the Supreme Court of the United States requires that briefs be typeset in Century.